CHOSEN
TO BE
CHALLENGED

Understanding the Question "Why Me"?

Cory A. Graves

Edited by: Meredeth D. Summers

CHOSEN TO BE CHALLENGED
Copyright © 2016 by Cre8iveSoul Publishing

All rights reserved. No part of this book may be reproduced or transmitted in any form or by any means without written permission from the author.

ISBN-10: 1537001035
ISBN-13: 978-1537001036

DEDICATION & ACKNOWLEDGMENTS

I would like to dedicate this first book to my parents, Floyd N. Graves and Hallie Summers Graves, as well as to my four sisters and five brothers, who have helped me make it through every challenge I've ever encountered.

A special "Thank You" to Meredeth Summers, one of the most gifted and humble persons I've ever had the pleasure of knowing.

CONTENTS

Preface

PREFACE

Have you ever wondered why certain things show up in your life at certain times? Have you ever asked the questions "why me" and "why now"? Well, the thing is, you probably have, because experiencing *life* is nothing new. If you are alive and breathing, then at some point you've come to realize that every day of your life can bring one or more challenges. These challenges come in many different facets and in many different ways. There isn't one particular area of your life that challenges target or prefer. I'm sure that you've experienced that challenges can show up in your body, your home, your workplace, and yes, even in your church. The reality is that no matter which area of your life is being challenged, it's important to remember that you have been CHOSEN to be challenged. As you read further, you'll find out exactly what this phrase means. It is my hope that this book will help you discover that no matter when or how you're challenged, the fact will always remain that the reason God allowed it was because He knew you could handle it.

1 SAMUEL 16:7 KJV

"But the LORD said unto Samuel, look not on his countenance, or on the height of his stature; because I have refused him: for the *LORD* seeth *not as man seeth; for man looketh on the outward appearance, but the LORD looketh on the heart."*

Chapter One

WHY WAS I CHOSEN FOR THIS?

Let's take a journey back in time. Take a moment to imagine when you were in elementary school on the playground. Remember when you used to play those games like kickball and dodge ball? Remember the day you got to be one of the "captains" and you could choose who you wanted on your team? As you looked over your classmates one by one, you were determining who you thought would be the best person to pick to ensure you had the winning team. Well, that's what God does when He is choosing you for the challenges you will face. He determines whether or not you are able to handle them. He selects you because He has looked around at many others and has determined that you are the person who will guarantee victory for His team. I know you may be saying to yourself, "there are others who are more qualified". I would totally disagree. Although others may appear to be more competent or capable, they simply are not who God wants. God isn't concerned with how we look and you shouldn't be either. We all know, or have heard, that looks can be deceiving. Are you familiar with the story of King David in the Bible? It all starts when we are introduced to him by Samuel in 1 Samuel, chapter 15. God sent the prophet Samuel to Bethlehem to find a king to rule over Israel. He did what God asked. He went to a man's house by the name of Jesse, a sheep herder who had seven sons. David was the youngest. When Samuel told Jesse the purpose of his visit, he asked Samuel to have each one of his boys come in front of him. The eldest of the sons came. He was a soldier with both experience and physique. Based solely upon this, they thought that he would be chosen to be the next king. But God told Samuel that he wasn't the one. In fact He said "man looks at the outward appearance, but God looks at the heart" (I Samuel 16:7 KJV). The same thing happened for each of Jesse's other sons until

Samuel asked for the only son that was left out of the seven. The last one was David. The Bible describes him as ruddy, with a fair countenance. No one would've ever suspected that David would be "chosen" to be the next king. However, God told Samuel that he was the one; this is the person that I've chosen to be king. David was actually the one that was chosen to be challenged. He didn't just go straight to the palace. Although his destiny had been determined, David had many challenges that he would encounter on his journey; and each one of those challenges would be imperative to him arriving at and being successful in his destiny. The same applies to you. God has predetermined your outcome, as well as the challenges that will help you get there. During the course of his journey, David would fight lions, bears, and giants that would more than triple him in size. He would even fight those whom he thought would be in his favor. Every challenge that David would encounter was necessary. Just like all of your challenges are necessary. Every challenge has a purpose. It grooms you for who you are destined to become. Each one leads you to a new level of maturity, reveals strength that you didn't even know you had, and deepens your faith and trust in God. If you are not challenged, you will never change. The truth of the matter is, the person you are before being challenged is quite different from the person you become afterwards. In fact, being chosen to be challenged should be considered a badge of honor. No one else has been equipped with the necessary tools, be it emotional, spiritual, or mental tools, to handle what you've been handpicked to endure. How awesome is that?!

Have you ever been told, "I don't know how you're able to handle all that without losing your mind? There's no way I could do it"! Guess what, they are telling the truth. They really don't know how you're able to handle it, and there's no way they could do it. Want to know why? I'll tell you. IT'S NOT THEIR CHALLENGE, it's yours. And it is designed especially for you. They were not equipped with the tools you were given in order to handle it. Remember that your challenges are designed to help you arrive at your destiny. Get past the challenge....arrive at your destiny.

1 CHRONICLES 15:20 KJV

"And he said, Hearken ye, all Judah, and ye inhabitants of Jerusalem, and thou king Jehoshaphat, Thus saith the LORD unto you, Be not afraid nor dismayed by reason of this great multitude; for the battle is not yours, but God's."

Chapter Two

HOW WILL I KNOW THAT I'M READY FOR MY CHALLENGE?

Let's go back to your elementary school playground one more time where you are the team captain. You're looking at your classmates trying to determine who could guarantee you a win. Think about it. There were those classmates of yours whom you chose without question and then there were those you avoided at all costs, right? This was based on past experience (like how you witnessed them perform at yesterday's recess), their strength, their size, and their skill. When we look at the things that God allows to challenge us, we often make the mistake of using these same criteria. We consider size, experience, strength and skill to determine whether or not we can handle the challenge. David was described as being small, nice looking and just a young boy whose only skill was looking after his father's sheep. Well, based off that description, no one would've ever thought that he could fight a lion, a bear, or a giant and actually win. Neither did David. What he had was faith, not in his own abilities, but in God's. The only way you'll ever know that you are ready for any challenges that arise in your life is based on your faith in an invincible God. When you allow God to fight what challenges you, with you, you will always be ready for any obstacle. Think about Jehoshaphat in the book of Chronicles. He was faced with all of his enemies plotting to come at him at the same time. He was frightened. His fear drove him to pray and get help from God. God's response was so powerful. He said to Jehoshaphat that this battle is not yours, it's the Lord's. What I'm trying to get you to understand is although God designs and allows your challenges, He doesn't necessarily want YOU to handle them alone. What comes as a result of your challenge (fear, frustration, helplessness) should drive you into prayer with God. He expects you to cry out to him for help, for comfort, and for direction during each of your challenges. God will give you what you need, when you need it. All too often we waste too much time trying to figure a way out of our trials. Many of our challenges as believers aren't allowed so that we can figure out how to get out of them, but they are allowed so that we can figure out how to get through them. I like to think of this as the "process". Going *through* our challenges reminds me of a caterpillar whose destiny at birth is to become a beautiful butterfly. In order for him to reach his destiny and become that beautiful butterfly that he was created to become, he has to make it through many challenges. The most extreme one is to make it through the stage of the cocoon.

Now while he is in that very tight "situation",
he is being transformed. He is slowly, but
surely, developing into what God created him
to be. His abilities, his countenance, and his
appearance change as a result of overcoming
his greatest challenge. If the caterpillar didn't
go through the entire process, just like we
must do, (I mean *it*), to fly would never
properly develop; which means that he could
never soar to his full potential, or even soar
at all. You have to complete the
process! Once the process is complete, so
too is the challenge. Remember, there is a
destiny that's awaiting you. In order for you
to reach that destiny, you have to make it
through your challenges. Doing so is simply
the process you'll need to prepare you for
what's awaiting you in your future. Every
challenge is set up to make you stronger,

wiser, and better. Your last challenge is what prepared you for your next challenge. The next chapter will help you better understand this assertion.

2 CHRONICLES 7:14 KJV

"If my people, which are called by my name, shall humble themselves, and pray, and seek my face, and turn from their wicked ways; then will I hear from heaven, and will forgive their sin, and will heal their land."

WHAT IF I CAN'T HANDLE MY CHALLENGE?

I Corinthians 10:13 NKJV says this: "no temptation has overtaken you but such as is common to man, but God is faithful who will not allow you to be tempted beyond what you are able". Simply put, God will never allow a challenge to come your way without first making sure you have what you need to make it through it. Let me explain it like this: let's go back to school for a moment. Remember when you were in grade school and how in order for you to pass from grade to grade you always had to take some kind of test? Well, the test that you had to take when you were in, let's just say third grade, was to 1 - make sure you understood all the third grade material and 2 - prepare you for the challenges of the fourth grade. Your teacher never gave you a fourth grade test while you were in the third grade. You weren't prepared nor equipped to handle it. You tested on "grade-level". The same concept applies with God. He won't give you a test/challenge that's above your spiritual grade-level. With that being said, every challenge that you encounter, you are prepared to make it through. If you feel that you cannot make it through, could it be that you've not paid attention in class? (i.e. Bible study, Sunday school, Sunday morning service, personal devotion time?...it's just a question). There's another important fact that you should know when it comes to making it through what challenges you. The challenge (your challenge) was allowed by God so that He can get glory from you. It wasn't allowed to make you look bad, go crazy, or lose it. It was allowed so that you, as you make it through, can allow people to witness the awesomeness of God's power at work in your life. He wouldn't get any glory out of the challenges He allowed in your life if they were more than you could handle. That not only makes you look bad, but it also makes God look bad. And God has no intention of ever looking bad at your expense. Anybody can talk about how good God is when everything is going well in their life. But it takes a true believer to talk about how good He is when things aren't going so well. A true believer knows that where they are today, doesn't mean that's where they'll be tomorrow. The other day I was watching my grandson Kameron, who is fifteen months old, trying for the first time to get down from off my bed (one of the many challenges that he's trying to overcome at his age). He had strategically mastered getting down off the couch and a couple of chairs, but the bed was a little higher. He followed the same process as he does trying to get off the couch, but there was something different and he knew it. His feet were dangling in the air and he couldn't touch the floor like he could while climbing down from the couch. He began to whimper a little and hang on to the sheets of the bed for dear life. What he didn't realize was that his feet were only about an inch from the floor. Was this challenge more than he could handle? Of course not! All he had to do was let go and the challenge that he thought was insurmountable, would have been conquered. However, I have to add that I did what any loving, caring grandfather would do. Once he started to whimper, I reached out my hand to make sure that he knew he was safe; just like God will do you when you think that you're in an unconquerable challenge. Your little whimper will cause Him to come to your rescue even if you're only inches away from victory. All God wants is for us to trust Him. One thing I've learned over the years, and it's seen throughout the Bible, is that God is a "contingency" God. That means He expects you to do something before He does something. For example, 2 Chronicles 7:14 KJV says, "if my people which are called by my name, shall humble themselves, and pray, and seek my face, and turn from their wicked ways" (that's what He expects us to do, then this is what He will do)... "I'll hear from heaven, forgive their sin, and heal their land". Sometimes God only wants us to face the challenge and then He'll fight the battle. Remember the only thing He wants from us is TRUST.

ROMANS 8:28 KJV

"And we know that all things work together for good to them that love God, to them who are the called according to his purpose."

DOES EVERY CHALLENGE HAVE A PURPOSE?

I am convinced that everything God allows to come in our lives to challenge us, whether it's a challenge with our finances, our relationships, or our health, for example, all have a purpose. As I stated in the

previous chapter, passing the third grade test
(challenge) is what prepares you for the
fourth grade. Whatever happens today is
what is needed to prepare you for
your tomorrow. If you can't handle the
challenges of your today, then how can you
handle the challenges of your tomorrow?
Your "now" is what prepares you for your
"next". The apostle Paul wrote to the church
at Rome in Romans 8:18 KJV, "for I reckon
that the suffering (challenges) of this present
time are not worthy to be compared to the
glory which shall be revealed in us". After
the challenge comes the big "reveal". You
should never come out of a challenging
situation the same way you went in to it.
Some things about you should change. The
very thing that challenges you should also
have the ability to change you. Now keep in

mind that it's completely up to you as to how you will change. You can choose to allow the challenge to make you bitter or allow it to make you better. The choice is yours. You can't forget that the challenge was allowed by God so that He could receive glory from you. It's only when you make it through your challenges that God gets the glory. That's when your test turns into a testimony; testify to everyone about how good God is. When you come out victoriously, it lets the whole world know that God is still God. However, He receives no glory if you allow the challenge to make you a bitter believer. I don't want to give you the impression that you will never have weak moments or even weak days. You will! There will be times when you will feel that your challenge is bigger than you are, bigger than your faith, maybe even bigger than your God. In fact, that's what the devil would love for you to think. But I'm certain you know that's not true. God is bigger than any challenge you will ever face. Isaiah wrote in chapter 43:2 KJV to encourage the people and let them know that there is nothing that they will go through that God will not be there to go through it with them. He said, "when thou passeth through the water, I'll be with thee; and through the rivers they shall not overflow thee: when thou walkest through the fire, thou shalt not be burned; neither shall the flame kindle upon thee". The only reason He brought you TO the challenge is to carry you THROUGH the challenge. God's promise to you as His child is that He is a present help in the time of trouble. He'll walk with you *in* what may challenge you, walk with you *through* what may challenge you, and He'll be with you when you come *out of* what challenges you. Guess what? You will come out!

"But thanks be to God, which giveth us the victory through our Lord Jesus Christ."

Chapter Five

THE MIND OF AN OVERCOMER

Do you have the mindset of a VICTOR or a VICTIM? Even though you are hand selected to go through each and every one of your challenges, it's still important for you to embrace them with the right mindset. The way you face your challenge will determine how you come out. Having a victor's mentality from the beginning means that you've already predetermined that whatever the problem, you will defeat it and not allow it to defeat you. Does that mean you won't have some weary days? Or, days where it seems like you want to just give up and throw in the towel? That's not what having a victor's mentality means at all. The truth is, no matter how strong you think you are, there will always be at least one challenge that has the ability to bring you to your knees. The victor's mentality, however, gives you the confidence to know that in spite of what it looks like, things will still work out in your favor. Remember, you were chosen for your challenge and your challenge was chosen for you. You and your challenge(s) were put together by the wisdom of God. He strategically and purposefully makes sure that you will have everything needed to make it through every pitfall, valley, mountain, and hurdle that comes along with your challenge. Knowing and believing means that you have a victor's mentality. Unfortunately, there's an opposite end of this spectrum. It's having the victim's mentality. I'm sure you're familiar with it. Many of us have had it at some point in our lifetime. Having the victim's mentality simply means that you have failed to recognize that the very thing that is challenging you IS the very thing that God is using to groom you. I know you may be thinking, "how can something that feels so bad, that depresses me, frustrates me and is seemingly tearing me apart be used to groom me?". Think about this. Have you ever worked out in a gym, or at least seen people who do? The muscles that they have developed came as a result of being ripped and torn. That's right, the harder the muscle has to work, the bigger, and stronger it will become, but only after it has experienced some ripping. The same principle applies to your spirit, as well as your faith. The more difficult the challenge is, the greater the yield. If you can't handle your challenges of today how can you recognize your blessings of tomorrow? Having the victim's mentality means that you've lost hope; hope that things can change, hope that things will work for your good, hope that God wouldn't bring you here to leave you here. Let me encourage you to do away with the victim's mentality and embrace the victor's mentality. If you face your challenges believing that 1 - God has orchestrated them and is in control of the situation; 2 - that your challenges are designed specifically for your level of emotional, spiritual, mental and even physical strength; and 3 - that your challenges of the present time are being used to groom you, develop you, and strengthen you for your next level, then you will come out of any challenge knowing that what was meant for evil, God turned into good for you. You should also realize that every time you are challenged, God is merely preparing you for something bigger, something greater. Your challenges should always inspire and empower you, because each one affords you the opportunity to tap into potential that you may have never realized you had. I admonish you from this day forward, whenever you're faced with a challenge, to first thank God for choosing you for the challenge, and then ask God, "how will this challenge bring you glory?". After all, it's not about you, it's about Him. He chose you to bring Him glory. Allow your test to turn into a testimony for Him.

About the Author

Cory A. Graves was born and raised in Brown Summit, North Carolina and currently resides in Colfax, North Carolina. He is a graduate of East Carolina University, where he majored in Special Education and Psychology. He is a former educator and currently serves as the Senior Pastor of White Oak Grove Missionary Baptist Church, located in Greensboro, North Carolina. He serves on several boards throughout the triad area that focuses on children and adults with mental and physical disabilities, as well as at risk youth and adolescents. He is the founder of a mentoring group known as SFC (Strong, Focused and Confident) that mentors African American boys and young men. He teaches that every challenge and/or adversity should be used as a reason to succeed, as opposed to an excuse to fail.

54568631R00024

Made in the USA
Columbia, SC
02 April 2019